Space Pioneers
ASTRONAUTS

Richard and Louise Spilsbury

Heinemann Library
Chicago, Illinois

© 2008 Heinemann Library
a division of Reed Elsevier Inc.
Chicago, Illinois

Customer Service 888-454-2279
Visit our Web site at www.heinemannraintree.com

Design: Richard Parker and Manhattan Design
Illustrations: Darren Lingard
Picture Research: Mica Brancic and Virginia Stroud-Lewis
Production: Alison Parsons

Originated by Modern Age
Printed and bound in China by Leo Paper Group

12 11 10 09 08
10 9 8 7 6 5 4 3 2 1

Library of Congress Cataloging-in-Publication Data

Spilsbury, Richard, 1963-
  Space pioneers : astronauts / Richard and Louise Spilsbury.
    p. cm. -- (Scientists at work)
  Includes bibliographical references and index.
  ISBN 978-1-403-49951-6 (hardback : alk. paper) -- ISBN 978-1-403-49958-5 (pbk. : alk. paper) 1. Astronautics--Vocational guidance--Juvenile literature. 2. Astronauts--Juvenile literature. I. Spilsbury, Louise. II. Title.
  TL850.S65 2007
  629.450023--dc22
                          2007012491

Acknowledgments
The publishers would like to thank the following for permission to reproduce photographs: ©Corbis pp. **10** & **11** (NASA/Roger Ressmeyer); **14**, **16**, **26** (Roger Ressmeyer); **18** (NASA/JPL/Handout/Reuters), **21** (Assignments Photographers/Bryn Colton), **24** (John Henley), **25** (Richard T. Nowitz); ©European Space Agency (ESA) p. **23**; ©Getty Images pp. **27** (AFP), **28-29** (Photodisc); ©NASA pp. **5**, **6**, **7**, **8** & **9** (Kennedy Space Center), **13** (Johson Space Center), **20**; ©Science Photo Library/NASA pp. **4**, **12**, **15**, **17**, **19** (ESA/STSCI/J. Hesher & P. Scowen, ASU), **22** (Roger Harris).

Cover photograph of a spacewalk reproduced with permission of Getty Images/PhotoDisc/StockTrek.

The publishers would like to thank Geza Gyuk for his assistance in the preparation of this book.

Every effort has been made to contact copyright holders of any material reproduced in this book. Any omissions will be rectified in subsequent printings if notice is given to the publishers.

Disclaimer
All the Internet addresses (URLs) given in this book were valid at the time of going to press. However, due to the dynamic nature of the Internet, some addresses may have changed, or sites may have changed or ceased to exist since publication. While the author and publishers regret any inconvenience this may cause readers, no responsibility for any such changes can be accepted by either the author or the publishers.

Contents

What Are Astronauts? 4

What Do Astronauts Do in Space? 10

What Is It Like To Live on a Spacecraft? 14

How Have Astronauts Changed Our Lives? 18

What Does It Take To Become an Astronaut? 24

Timeline of Space Travel 28

Glossary 30

Find Out More 31

Index 32

Any words appearing in the text in bold, **like this**,
are explained in the Glossary.

What Are Astronauts?

Astronauts are people who travel into space. Space is the gap between Earth and everything else in the **universe**. Astronauts go into space to study our **solar system**. This is made up of the sun (our nearest **star**) and eight **planets**, including Earth. It also includes other objects, such as the moon. Astronauts also study how living in space is different from living on Earth. Astronauts may visit space for just a few days or sometimes many months at a time.

In space

Space begins roughly 60 miles (100 kilometers) above Earth's surface. This is where the **atmosphere**, the band of gases surrounding Earth, ends. Space is not completely empty. It contains very small amounts of floating dust, gas, and pieces of rock of various sizes. The large rocks that move around the sun are called **asteroids**. When small, fast-moving pieces of space rock fly into Earth's atmosphere they burn up. These are called meteors.

This is a telecommunication satellite orbiting Earth. The equipment it carries allows people around the world to send each other phone and e-mail messages.

The space age

Before humans went into space, animals were used to determine whether space travel was safe for living things. In 1957 a dog was sent into space, followed by a monkey in 1959. The first astronauts went into space in 1961. By 1969 technology had advanced enough to send astronauts to the moon, which is approximately 240,000 miles (385,000 kilometers) away. Since the 1980s, astronauts have taken many machines, such as **satellites**, into space. Satellites are left in space to **orbit** (circle) Earth. They carry useful equipment, such as devices that track the changing weather on our planet.

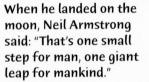

When he landed on the moon, Neil Armstrong said: "That's one small step for man, one giant leap for mankind."

WHO'S WHO: Yuri Gagarin and Neil Armstrong

The first person in space was Yuri Gagarin, a **cosmonaut** (the Russian word for astronaut). He spent almost two hours in space on April 12, 1961. It was the United States, however, who won the race to put the first astronaut on the moon. On July 20, 1969, U.S. astronaut Neil Armstrong took his first steps on the moon's surface.

Traveling to space

Astronauts and **spacecraft** travel to space using **rockets**. These are vehicles that burn **fuel** to blow gases out behind them. This makes the rocket move forward. Rockets sent into space have large **masses**. This is because they not only carry astronauts and their equipment, but also have heavy engines and tanks full of fuel. Anything with a mass is pulled back toward Earth's surface by the force of **gravity**. In order to overcome gravity and stay in space, rockets need to move at speeds faster than 16,700 miles per hour (25,200 kilometers per hour).

Most rockets are used for just one trip into space. They are made in parts (called stages) and each rocket has an engine and fuel. During the launch, once one stage has finished **thrusting** it falls off the rocket and is destroyed. The next stage then takes over. In 1981 the first reusable spacecraft, called a **space shuttle**, was launched. Shuttles blast off with the help of rockets, but astronauts can fly them back to Earth for use on other space missions.

Rockets like this use some of the most powerful engines ever made to reach space. The thrust is approximately 50 times that of a jumbo jet.

Staying in space

The pull of gravity in space is much weaker than in the atmosphere because Earth is farther away. Astronauts orbiting Earth don't feel the pull of gravity. This is because although they are constantly falling toward Earth, their high speed lets them miss Earth and keep orbiting. Spacecraft typically travel at roughly 18,000 miles per hour (29,000 kilometers per hour) in orbit. This high speed slows their gradual fall toward Earth.

The space shuttle is a vehicle that can transport things and people between Earth and space.

The science behind it: Feeling light

Just like you feel weightless if you're jumping on a trampoline, astronauts in space don't feel any weight. This is called **microgravity**. Weight is the force of gravity on a mass. Microgravity lets astronauts and objects float around in space.

Long training

Becoming an astronaut takes many years of training. Astronauts in space can be several hundred miles from Earth. They also live in very different conditions from those they are used to. They have to operate complicated and expensive equipment. It takes time to learn the job and how to deal calmly with any problems that could occur, such as equipment failures. Many astronaut trainees already have jobs, such as being a doctor or a pilot, that have taught them useful skills for life in space.

Thousands of people apply but only about 100 actually train as astronauts each year. Of these 100, about 10 people are chosen to be astronauts. Even then it can take years before they actually get to go into space. Space missions are very expensive and don't happen very often. Only about 500 people have ever been to space.

During astronaut training, people get used to using equipment on Earth that they will use when they get to space.

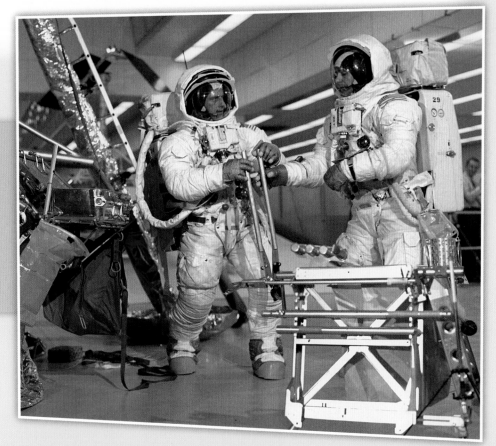

Hundreds of people work on a space mission, but only a handful leave Earth's atmosphere.

On the ground

What do trained astronauts do when they aren't in space? They often become part of a **ground crew** for a space mission. The ground crew is the large group of people on Earth who help the people in space. They may prepare spacecraft for flight, use powerful computers to monitor and help control the craft, and communicate with astronauts in space. Astronauts may work with the ground crew to develop space experiments. They may work with engineers who design spacecraft. Their knowledge of what the ground crew can do is very helpful when they do have the chance to go into space.

WHO'S WHO: John Glenn

John Glenn was first a World War II pilot and then an astronaut. In 1962 he became the first American to orbit Earth. Thirty-six years later, after working as a politician, he went to space again. In 1998, at the age of 77, Glenn became the oldest person ever to go into space.

What Do Astronauts Do in Space?

Astronauts go into space with careful plans about which tasks need to be performed and by whom. These tasks can range from piloting a space shuttle to fixing a satellite. They rely on their equipment in order to do their work properly.

Types of astronaut

Astronauts in a spacecraft crew have different roles. The commander is in charge of the success and safety of a mission, and the pilot controls and operates the spacecraft. One or several mission specialists carry out experiments and leave the craft to go out into space. They are also in charge of the **payload** (cargo). This is all the equipment carried on a particular mission.

The pilot has specialized knowledge of the instruments controlling the speed, altitude, and direction of a spacecraft.

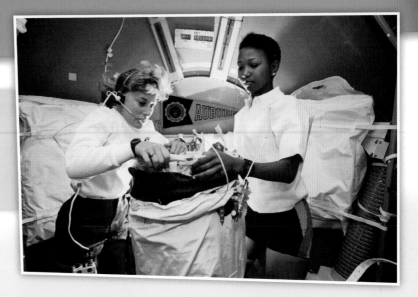

Scientific work

Every mission requires that astronauts perform certain experiments. Many experiments test the effects of microgravity on growth and chemical reactions. For example, the roots of plants grow downward on Earth but not in space. Candle flames burn as blue circles in space. Both of these differences are because of the different strength of gravity. Astronauts also put satellites into orbit that can send useful scientific information back to Earth. For example, the Hubble **Space Telescope** was the payload on a 1990 shuttle mission. This powerful telescope in orbit can see distant **galaxies** in great detail.

Repairs

Astronauts often make repairs to satellites and other objects in orbit. For example, Hubble's images were blurry when the telescope was first put in space. Astronauts on a later mission used a **robotic arm** to grab the telescope and add a piece to it. This made the images clearer. Astronauts may also make minor repairs when rocks moving through space damage spacecraft.

WHO'S WHO: Ellen Ochoa

Ellen Ochoa was the first Hispanic woman in space. She invented artificial eyes that robots use to recognize objects. She used her robot experience when she became a mission specialist on three space shuttle missions. Ochoa operated a robotic arm that put into orbit and grabbed satellites that study the sun's effects on Earth's climate.

Building projects

Astronauts also need to have building skills. **Space stations** are large spacecraft permanently in orbit. Different astronauts can live and work on them for periods of time. Most space stations are too big to send whole from Earth, so astronauts on different missions bring up the various parts and put them together piece by piece. When it is completed, the International Space Station will be as big as a soccer field and weigh 500 tons (510 metric tons). It should be completed by 2010, after more than 40 missions.

The first part of the International Space Station, which was put into orbit in 1998, is marked with an arrow. The other parts were added over the next two years. It is now much bigger.

Spacesuits

Astronauts sometimes need to leave the shuttle or station and go out into space to perform repairs. They can only do this if they put on a spacesuit that provides the right environment for them to survive.

Spacesuits help keep astronauts at the right temperature and pressure. In space, it gets boiling hot in the sun and freezing in the shade. Spacesuits are white to reflect heat. They also have thin water tubes inside to carry heat away from the skin. On Earth, the atmosphere pushes against our bodies and holds us together. In space, with no **air pressure**, our bodies would swell up and damage our organs. Air is pumped through the suit to keep the pressure up. This makes the suit somewhat difficult to bend, except at the joints.

Spacesuits allow astronauts to survive and work outside the spacecraft.

TRICKS OF THE TRADE: SPACE WALK REMINDERS

Take your backpack! An astronaut's backpack contains enough air to last for a seven-hour space walk. We need to breathe the **oxygen** in air to live. There is no air and no oxygen in space, so astronauts carry their own supply.

Don't let go of nuts and bolts! Spacesuit gloves are big and difficult to grip with, but remember that anything you drop stays in orbit. Spacecraft travel very fast, and even tiny objects can puncture holes in spacecraft if they collide with them.

What Is It Like To Live on a Spacecraft?

Microgravity makes living in space very different from living on Earth. Everyday activities, such as eating and bathing, are not the same in space.

Eating

Astronauts have no refrigerators because they don't work well in microgravity conditions. Refrigerators also use too much electricity. Astronauts' food is preserved in other ways, such as in canned or dried form. They have ovens to warm food and water to add to dried food, such as powdered soup.

Astronauts have to be careful about spilling crumbs of food and drops of drinks. These may float away and could possibly damage equipment. Astronauts often eat foods that don't make crumbs, such as casseroles or chili. They eat from plastic containers with lids, and drink from sealed foil pouches. They also use straps to hold down food and drink containers during meals.

The main difference between your food and drink and an astronaut's is that theirs must be kept in containers and bottles to keep it from floating around.

TOOLS OF THE TRADE: FAVORITE SPACE FOODS

Tortillas: unlike normal bread they stay fresh a long time and produce very few crumbs

Packaged snacks: nuts, dried fruit, cookies, and pepperoni

Condiments: condiments such as spicy sauce are used to flavor food. Salty water and peppery oil are splashed on food because salt or pepper grains would float away.

Hygiene

Most spacecraft, such as the space stations, must carry enough water to last an entire mission. This means astronauts must use as little water as possible. They wash with damp washcloths and sponges. They use special toilets that flush away waste using air instead of water. They use disposable food containers, and they even wear disposable clothes instead of clothing that needs to be washed. However, astronauts on shuttles are able to shower. The dirty water is sucked away by a machine.

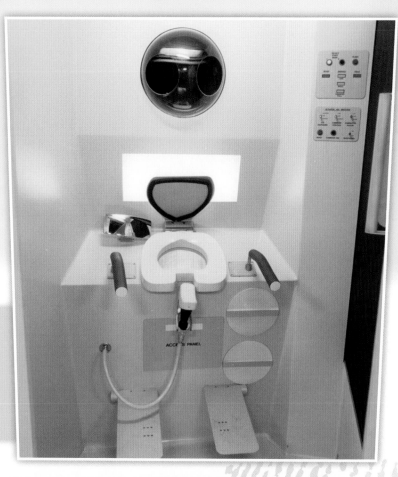

A space toilet has handles that astronauts grip to keep themselves from floating off the seat when they are using it.

Relaxation

Astronauts sleep in sleeping bags strapped into beds to prevent them from floating away. Night time is noisy because they need to sleep by electric fans. These fans blow the **carbon dioxide** gas the astronauts breathe out away from their faces. This is necessary because carbon dioxide is poisonous when it builds up in air. On Earth, natural air movements waft carbon dioxide away from our noses and mouths, but the air moves too slowly in a spacecraft.

Keeping moving

Astronauts do not have a lot of room to walk or run around, since spacecraft are often crowded. They spend half an hour each day cycling on exercise bikes, running on treadmills, or using rowing machines to keep their bodies strong and healthy. Staying active is important for good health. When astronauts are not active, fluids inside them build up in their heads. This causes "space sniffles," which is similar to a cold.

In microgravity conditions, astronauts may sleep vertically. This astronaut is typing messages to her family on Earth while tied into her sleeping bag.

Life support

Astronauts keep a close watch on the onboard equipment that preserves their environment. They check on amounts of oxygen being added to the air they breathe. They check on air filters that remove carbon dioxide from the air. They also check on water supplies. Most spacecraft have systems for recycling water. For example, filters remove waste from water vapor people breathe out and from **urine**, so the water can be used again. On the International Space Station, machines capture 53 pounds (24 kilograms) of water from the air each day.

Staying healthy is important for astronauts. It keeps their muscles from getting weaker because of weightlessness.

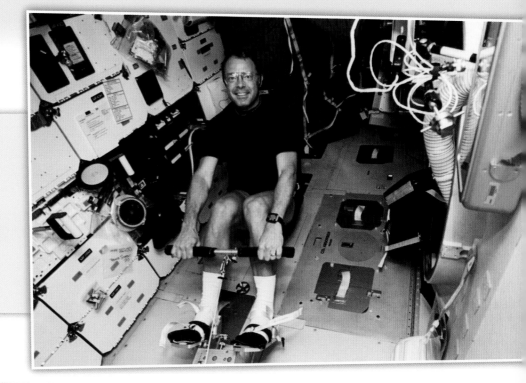

The science behind it: Bodies in space

Without exercise, astronauts' bones and muscles get lighter and weaker. On Earth, muscles and bones work together to support the weight of our bodies as we move around. This keeps them strong. **Weightlessness** in space means this doesn't happen. Astronauts also get up to two inches (five centimeters) taller during a space mission. This is caused when the bones in their backs stretch due to the lack of body weight pushing them together. The astronauts return to normal size soon after returning to Earth.

How Have Astronauts Changed Our Lives?

The *Sojourner* was an unmanned robot vehicle that explored the surface of Mars for 83 days in 1997. Its cameras took more than 17,000 pictures of the planet.

Astronauts have had many effects on our lives. They have helped us understand space. They have also helped develop new technologies we use on Earth.

Exploring the unknown

Astronauts on spacecraft and unmanned missions into space have taught us a lot about our solar system. **Probes** are unmanned craft that send data and collect samples from distant space. For example, the probe *Giotto* flew close enough to fast-moving comets to confirm they are made of rock and ice. The probe *Galileo* investigated the poisonous gases in the atmosphere above Jupiter. In 2004 robot vehicles called *Spirit* and *Opportunity* landed on and explored parts of the surface of Mars. They discovered that there was once water on the planet. The United States is planning for international manned missions to Mars in the future.

Telling the world

Many people are fascinated by space. Astronauts bring back rock samples, photos, and information to show scientists—and also the public. There are many displays and exhibits about space in museums and at colleges and universities. Astronauts sometimes give lectures and talks in schools about their fascinating experiences on spacecraft.

Publicity is important to encourage young people to study hard and become the astronauts of the future. Public interest in space exploration could also help encourage governments to pay for expensive new missions.

Images taken by the Hubble Space Telescope have helped us learn about distant galaxies.

WHO'S WHO: Edwin Hubble

Edwin Hubble was a U.S. astronomer who worked in the first half of the 20th century. Using measurements of the size and speed of distant galaxies, Hubble figured out that the universe is expanding. Later scientists used Hubble's name on a space telescope. On Earth, the atmosphere blurs the view of distant objects. In space, the telescope is above Earth's atmosphere. Astronomers today can see the universe much more clearly than Hubble ever could.

Space medicine

Technology developed for spacecraft has been used to help sick people. Engineers used ideas from a space shuttle fuel pump to develop an artificial heart for people with heart disease. Engineers have also used the light, hard material developed to protect shuttle fuel tanks to make better **prosthetic** limbs. Special lights used to grow plants in space labs are now used to treat certain brain diseases in children.

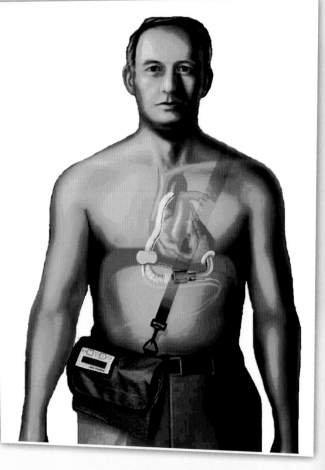

This artificial heart pumps blood through a person whose heart doesn't work. The pump uses space technology to make sure blood flows properly through the machine.

Making improvements

Work by astronauts has helped companies improve the way they make things. For example, microgravity experiments helped scientists make larger and better quality silicon chips. These chips are used to make computers and many other electronic machines work. The bouncy soles of modern tennis shoes have better grip, fit, and springiness than shoes of the past. They are made using technology first designed to make spacesuit helmets.

New gadgets

Spacecraft and other space equipment are crammed with new technology that can be useful on Earth. For example, cordless drills were first developed to help astronauts work while on the moon. Sensitive cameras used to detect rays in space can also be used to spot forest fires from long distances. Software used to get clear images of the space shuttle may be used to make better home videos.

This firefighter is holding a special camera designed to help locate the hottest parts of fires. The camera's technology was developed for space missions.

The science behind it: Stopping asteroids

Asteroids are large pieces of rock in space. Some have hit Earth in the past. These impacts have killed animals and plants and have affected the weather. Astronauts may be sent on a mission to stop future asteroids heading for Earth. They plan to attach engines to the asteroids to thrust them away from our planet.

An astronaut's life

Jim Reilly, a U.S. astronaut, believes that his job is a bit like being a builder. On a mission, he may spend days connecting power lines, lifting supplies, making sure satellites are working, and bolting pieces on to spacecraft. It is also a dangerous place to work and requires a lot of concentration to keep safe. For example, turning a bolt too hard could push an astronaut away from the craft and into space. You always have to think about what you are doing and ask yourself "do I need to do this task a little slower?" While working, however, astronauts can easily forget what a remarkable place space is. One of Reilly's favorite memories is leaning out of the spacecraft and then swinging out with just one hand on the space station so he could look across the Earth.

Imagine how it would feel looking down at Earth from space.

André Kuipers carried out 21 experiments during his stay on the International Space Station.

Space experiments

André Kuipers is a Dutch astronaut who went to space in 2004. Here are some of the experiments he worked on during one day of his mission.

Plant growth: André planted some lettuce seeds at the exact same time as students back in the Netherlands and videotaped how they grew. The students could then see how gravity affected plant growth on Earth.

Blood flow: This was a test of how heart rate and blood flow changed in space. On Earth, this varies by night and day. In space, there may be several light and dark parts of each day because the spacecraft is orbiting Earth, so the pattern changed.

Up or down?: André tested a special vest that buzzes inside to show which way is up and which is down. Spacecraft are color-coded to help astronauts distinguish up from down, but it is easy to get disorientated because of microgravity. This technology could also be useful to firefighters working in thick smoke.

What Does It Take To Become an Astronaut?

Do you ever dream of visiting another planet, traveling in space, or living on a space station? If so, then becoming an astronaut could be the job for you.

Astronomical telescopes help you pick out details in space that a normal telescope or binoculars would not be able to spot.

Learning more

Learn about space by looking at it. Try observing the night sky using a telescope. You can find more about the things you see in the sky by reading books, watching TV shows, and looking at Internet sites.

Visit places that have displays about space. These include planetariums, which are special theaters with models or movies of our solar system. You may be lucky enough to visit a space center, with real spacecraft on display. Many young astronomers join clubs or societies to meet other space enthusiasts.

Study hard

You will have to study science and math at school and college to become an astronaut. For example, physics will help you understand microgravity and how other planets are different from Earth. Math will help you calculate orbits. If you hope to become a pilot of a spacecraft, you will need to learn how to fly and command airplanes. There are many other important skills that will help you as an astronaut, such as the ability to work as part of a team.

Young people staying at Space Camp may even get to command realistic spacecraft simulators.

TRICKS OF THE TRADE: SPACE CAMP

Many budding astronauts have attended Space Camp in Huntsville, Alabama. It is a place where kids learn about space, spacecraft, robots, and being an astronaut—and also have a lot of fun. There are special machines that spin you around in different directions so you can feel disorientated. There are other machines that allow you to experience what it is like walking on the moon. Older kids can join a space academy where they get to do more challenging activities.

The next best thing

People selected to train to be astronauts study at special space academies, such as Johnson Space Center in the United States and Star City in Russia. This gives them the chance to practice working in conditions similar to those in space.

There are two ways for people to practice what it is like in space. One way to practice is underwater. The trainees put on spacesuits that neither sink nor float and go into huge water tanks. They move in and around life-sized models of parts of the space shuttle or other spacecraft to practice using them. The other way to feel what it is like in space is on a special airplane. This plane flies up and down through the sky over and over again. This creates microgravity conditions for a few seconds at the top of each arc. It feels a bit like being on a very long, steep rollercoaster ride.

Trainee astronaut pilots also use computer simulators to practice flying to and in space. The simulators have flight controls just like real spacecraft, but instead of windows to the outside they have computer screens. These show different scenes, so the trainees feel like they are really steering the craft.

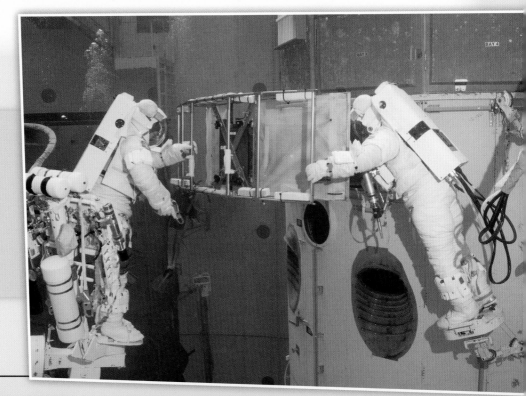

Astronauts carry out tasks underwater to prepare for real missions in outer space.

Passengers in *SpaceShipTwo* will be carried high into the atmosphere underneath a special airplane before blasting off into space.

Space tourists

In the future, people may be able to get to space with just a few days of training. Some private companies, such as Virgin Galactic, are developing spacecraft that can take tourists to view Earth from space. Passengers will also be able to experience a few minutes of weightlessness. Fully trained astronauts will operate the craft. The problem is that the tickets will be very expensive, and the trips will last less than three hours from start to finish.

The science behind it: Living on Mars

Some scientists believe that in the distant future people may be able to live on other planets, such as Mars. The problem is that Mars' atmosphere is very thin and made up of mostly carbon dioxide. If astronauts could build sealed domes on Mars and control the conditions inside, people could one day live there. Scientists might then gradually change the entire atmosphere on Mars to one in which people, and other living creatures, could survive without being inside a dome. They would do this by releasing gases from the surface of Mars to make the atmosphere thicker. They would also introduce green plants to turn carbon dioxide in Mars' atmosphere into oxygen.

Timeline of Space Travel

October 1957:
Sputnik 1 becomes world's first satellite. The 183-pound (83-kilogram) Russian spacecraft orbits Earth every 98 minutes.

November 1957:
Laika the dog is the first animal in space aboard *Sputnik 2*

December 1962:
Mariner 2 is the first spacecraft to reach another planet when it gets to Venus after a three-month journey

February 1966:
An unmanned Moon landing by *Luna 9* spacecraft

April 1971:
Russian *Salyut* becomes the world's first space station

November 1971:
Mariner 9 enters orbit around another planet, Mars. Its photos of the surface include 20 volcanoes, one of them bigger than any on Earth.

1950s

1960s

1970s

April 1961:
Yuri Gagarin becomes the first cosmonaut (Russian astronaut) when he goes into orbit around Earth

March 1965:
Alexei Leonov takes the first space walk

July 1969:
Apollo 11 lands on the moon with astronauts on board. Neil Armstrong is the first astronaut to walk on its surface.

May 1973:
U.S. *Skylab* space station goes into orbit

December 1973:
Pioneer 10 reaches Jupiter, our solar system's largest planet

July 1976:
Viking is the first spacecraft to land on Mars

April 1981:
The first space shuttle mission

May 1989:
Magellan probe is launched from space shuttle in orbit around Earth. It soon enters orbit around Venus.

1994:
A shuttle mission to repair Hubble costs U.S. $630 million

January 2004:
Opportunity robot vehicle lands on the surface of Mars and starts driving across it

1980s

1990s

2000s

1977:
Voyager 1 is launched, heading for deep space

March 1986:
Giotto probe passes through the tail of Halley's Comet

1990:
Hubble Space Telescope is carried into space aboard a space shuttle

November 1998:
The first part of the International Space Station goes into orbit

August 2006:
Voyager 1 probe now 100 times farther than Earth from the sun and nearing the edge of our solar system

Glossary

air pressure push of air on the surface of objects

asteroid large chunk of rock in the solar system

atmosphere layer of gases around a planet such as Earth, held in place by gravity

carbon dioxide type of gas found in air, breathed out by humans and other animals

cosmonaut Russian astronaut

fuel substance that is burned to release heat and/or gas that makes vehicles and other machines move

galaxy huge system of stars, dust, and gases held together by gravity

gravity force pulling objects with mass together

ground crew team on the ground that supports astronauts during missions

mass amount of material in an object

microgravity very weak gravity that creates a feeling of weightlessness in astronauts

orbit curved path or journey that is taken around another object in space

oxygen gas in air that we need to breathe in order to live

payload cargo carried to space on a rocket

planet large sphere of rock or gas orbiting the sun or other star

probe unmanned spacecraft used to explore and record space

prosthetic artificial. Prosthetics are human-made body parts.

robotic arm device for grabbing and lifting heavy things, operated by people

rocket vehicle powered by rocket engines used to get spacecraft into space

satellite object held in orbit by gravity. Some satellites are made by people and put into space to view planets.

solar system the sun and all the planets, asteroids, and comets that orbit (circle) it

space shuttle reusable spacecraft that carries astronauts and cargo into space

space station large spacecraft that remains in orbit and is used by many astronauts over several years

space telescope instrument in space used to observe distant planets and galaxies

spacecraft vehicle put into space to explore the universe. Some carry astronauts while others only carry instruments.

star enormous ball of burning gas

thrust forward push

universe everything that exists including space and all the objects in it

urine waste water removed from your body when you go to the bathroom

weightlessness feeling that there is no pull of gravity on a mass

Find Out More

Further reading

Iverson, Teresa. *Ellen Ochoa*. Chicago: Raintree, 2006.

Simon, Seymour. *Earth: Our Planet in Space.* New York: Simon & Schuster, 2003.

Simon, Seymour. *Our Solar System.* New York: Harper Collins, 2007.

Solway, Andrew. *Can We Travel to the Stars?: Space Flight and Space Exploration.* Chicago: Heinemann Library, 2006.

Stott, Carole. *Stars and Planets*. Boston: Kingfisher, 2005.

Thompson, Sarah L. *Astronauts and Other Space Heroes.* New York: Harper Collins, 2007.

Websites

There are a lot of space activities to try out and fascinating facts at http://quest.arc.nasa.gov/index.html (including a virtual space experiment on flies!) and http://spaceplace.jpl.nasa.gov/en/kids/amazing_facts.shtml

Find out about Space Camp at http://www.spacecamp.com. There are details about the various programs offered for different ages and abilities, and how to enroll.

Have you ever wondered what Earth looks like from space? Visit http://eol.jsc.nasa.gov/sseop/EFS/categories.htm to find a clickable map and get an astronaut's view.

Check on the progress of the International Space Station and upcoming astronaut missions at http://www.nasa.gov/mission_pages/station/main/index.html

View some of the wonders of the universe, many captured using the Hubble Space Telescope, learn about telescopes, and even get some homework help at http://amazing-space.stsci.edu

Index

air pressure 13
animals in space 5, 28
Armstrong, Neil 5, 28
artificial hearts 20
asteroids 4, 21
astronauts
    becoming an astronaut 24-7
    famous astronauts 5, 9,
        11, 15
    life on a spacecraft 14-17,
        22-3
    training 8, 26-7
    types of astronaut 10
astronomical telescopes 11,
    19, 24
atmosphere 4, 13, 22, 27

blood flow experiments 23
building skills 12

carbon dioxide 16, 17, 27
comets 18
commanders 10
computer simulators 26
cordless drills 21

experiments in space 9, 11, 23

firefighting technology 21, 23
fitness and exercise 16, 17
food in space 14

Gagarin, Yuri 5, 28
galaxies 11, 19
Glenn, John 9
gravity 6, 7, 11, 23
ground crews 9

Hubble, Edwin 19
Hubble Space Telescope 11,
    19, 29

hygiene 15

information, publicizing 19
International Space Station 12,
    17, 23, 29

Johnson Space Center 26
Jupiter 18, 28

Kuipers, André 23

Mars 18, 27, 28, 29
mass 6, 7
meteors 4
microgravity 7, 11, 14, 20, 23,
    25, 26
Mir space station 15
moon 4, 5, 28

Ochoa, Ellen 11
orbit 5, 9, 12, 13, 23, 25
oxygen 13, 17, 27

payload 10, 11
pilots 10, 25, 26
planetariums 24
planets 4, 18, 27, 28
plant experiments 11, 23
Polyakov, Valeri 15
probes 18, 29
prosthetic limbs 20
public interest in space 19

Reilly, Jim 22
repairs 11, 13
robotic arm 11
rockets 6

satellites 4, 5, 10, 11, 22, 28
school and college subjects
    25

silicon chips 20
sleeping in space 16
solar system 4, 18, 24
space 4
space academies 25, 26
Space Camp 25
space medicine 20
space missions 10-13
space shuttles 6, 7, 10, 20,
    26, 29
"space sniffles" 16
space stations 12, 15, 17, 22,
    23, 28, 29
space technology, uses of 20-1
space tourists 27
space travel timeline 28-9
space walks 13, 22, 28
spacecraft 6, 7, 9, 10, 12, 14-17,
    24, 26, 27
SpaceShipOne 29
SpaceShipTwo 27
spacesuits 13, 20
Spirit robot vehicle 18
Star City 26

tennis shoes 20
toilets 15

underwater training 26
universe 4, 19
unmanned robot vehicles 18, 29
up from down, distinguishing 23

Venus 28, 29
videos 21

water supplies 15, 17
weightlessness 7, 17, 27